# Stopping By My Heart On A Fearless Day

## My Authentic Expression

Donna E. Saavedra

BookLeaf Publishing

India | USA | UK

Made with ❤ on the BookLeaf Publishing Platform
www.bookleafpub.in
www.bookleafpub.com

# Dedication

To my beloved children,
This book is for you. I have always dreamed of being a poet, and with this, my second book, I hope to inspire you to pursue your own dreams. Remember, dreams do come true, no matter how long it takes. Never give up on making them a reality.

To my wonderful husband, Peter,
Your unwavering support and encouragement have been my guiding light. Your love has meant the world to me throughout this journey and throughout my life. Thank you for giving me wings to fly.

To Tina,
We did it. Again! Keep writing and keep fighting. You've got this!

# Preface

From a young age, I have been captivated by the worlds
of reading, writing, and poetry. I often dreamed of
joining the ranks of literary greats like Ralph Waldo
Emerson, Edgar Allan Poe, and my all-time favorite,
Robert Frost. My aspirations included crafting children's
books that would resonate through time, akin to classics
like *Charlotte's Web* and *The Tale of Peter Rabbit*.
Ultimately, my desire was simply to write.

Writing became my primary means of authentic
expression, allowing me to convey my innermost
feelings. While I have explored spoken word, I find that
writing remains a more genuine outlet for me. The
poems I create serve to share my true emotions, even
when they may be challenging for some to read. My
hope is that they might inspire or resonate with others in
a meaningful way.

Vulnerability has always posed a challenge for me,
which is another reason I turn to writing. Through this
process, I uncover my true self and gain clarity on my
feelings. I encourage everyone to take a moment to grab
a pen and paper, or a computer, and engage in free
writing about any aspect of your life or emotions that

weigh heavily on you. Allow yourself to explore what emerges, distinguishing between your authentic voice and external influences.

In my poetry, I prefer to write without any rigid structure in mind. I like to see what and how the words come out. If you choose to write a poem, focus less on rhyme, stanzas, or form, and instead write freely and without constraints. Unless, you enjoy structure. Most importantly, write from the heart and embrace your true, authentic self.

# Acknowledgements

I would like to express my heartfelt gratitude to those who inspire me every day: my husband, Peter, and my children, Sebastian, Ethan, and Aubrey. Thank you for providing me with the space to pursue my dreams. Your unwavering support, love, and encouragement have been instrumental in my decision to take the leap into publishing my emotions.

To my dearest friend, Tina, thank you for being a constant beacon of inspiration and love. Your guidance and encouragement throughout this journey, have meant the world to me. You are a beautiful person, inside and out, and I look forward to collaborating and supporting one another in many more literary projects to come.

And to all my loved ones, family and friends, you have all been a source of inspiration to me throughout the years and my writing journey. Thank you for being in my life.

With all my love: Donna, Donnalou, Mom, Mama, Mommy, Friend

# 1. If No One Were Looking

If no one were looking, I just might cry...
I would cry all of the tears I was told as a child not to
release
I would let the salt run down my wounds feeling the
burn like fire until they healed.
I would let the river banks overflow into the oceans
taking with it all that had me drowning.

If no one were looking, I just might scream...
I would release the pains and fears that have gripped me
my whole life holding me down with the chains of
shame.
I would clear my lungs, my heart, and my soul of
unnecessary weight
And free myself from those burdens I let weigh me
down.

If no one were looking, I just might break down...
I would allow myself to feel every last nerve of every
emotion I was told not to feel.
I would release every last bit to create room for what
really matters.
I would allow self love to wash over all of the self doubt I
let control me.

If no one were looking, I would demand that they did...
So they can see my true strength and my innate
preciousness.
So they can watch as the ancestral chords break away
because they no longer serve me
And the woman I was meant to be and truly am.

While everyone is looking, I will be my authentic self...
I will cry and scream when I feel like it, unashamed.
I will dance in the streets and in the rain to the music of
life and love.
And I will just be me whether you look or not.

# 2. Stopping by My Heart On a Fearless Day

Whose heart is this, I think I know.
Her soul is trapped elsewhere though;
She cannot feel me waiting here
To help her heal her fragile soul.

My inner girl might think it severe,
To come out when there's so much fear.
Between the yesterdays and today,
The dark is always lurking near.

She shakes her head with words to say
To ask if she will be okay.
The only other sound's she weeps
Of strength for love and play.

My heart is lovely, dark and deep.
But I have promises to her and myself to keep,
And it's time for us to love and live so deep,
And it's time for us to love and live so deep.

# 3. Monsoon

Catalytic Energy
Clouds heavy with hope
The temperature suddenly drops
The sky booms
The earth shakes
Darkness looms
Fire ignites the sky
Power released
Water pours down
Cacti reach tall
Dry land drenched
Plants dance in the wind
Quickly it's over
The earth settles
All is still

# 4. The Vastness of Estrangement

In Loving Memory of My Father
Miguel Angel Castillo
10/23/1960 - 08/14/2024


It's an interesting thing when it comes to estrangement
and not at all what I expected
For one, you always think there is still time, until the
clock suddenly stops

Or, that the lack of connection means it won't hurt as
much
That the space between will somehow be enough to
absorb any and all pain

Your mind somehow convinces your heart that
everything will be easier to bare
And the walls you've built around your soul are stronger
than they actually are

However, when the estrangement becomes final and
death has taken away any chance of reconciliation
The walls you thought were impenetrable come crashing
down even harder creating an unbearable pain

An unbearable pain filled with grief, anger, sadness, and
longing...
Just a greater extension of what was already being felt
from years past

The already vast void of longing fractures even wider
during the earthquake of emotions
And you realize that what you felt before, was only the
tip of the iceberg

As the blast of icy cold air of sadness and grief hit you
like a ton of bricks
You're left with emotions that continue miles and miles
below the cold surface

No matter the length of the distance or the reasons why
Death during estrangement leaves an unimaginable
vacancy

A vacancy that will never be filled with reconciliation
but of unspoken words
A forever imprint of what was lost and what could have
been

I sit here listening to the breeze, looking for signs your
soul is trying to find mine

And, I find myself drowning in guilt as waves of panic
and sadness wash over me

Guilt for not pushing you harder or trying more
Even though I know I gave so much, leaving so little
emotionally, for my own family and I

Over two years ago I forgave you and told you I loved
you no matter what
I had no idea it would be our final interaction and our
last goodbye

I take solace knowing I shared my honest feelings and
love with you
Yet, hold sadness for the words you couldn't speak back

And, now, I know I will never hear those words spoken
by you
I'll never feel another strong hug from you

I won't get to hear you laugh or the jokes you told that
you thought were funny
And, there will be no more memories made of you and I
or you with your grandkids

I can choose to be angry and resentful and shout from
the rooftops at the top of my lungs

And let decades of locked up emotions and tears stream
down my face

I can choose to beat myself up with grief and guilt
wondering if I should have tried harder
Even though I gave so much time and energy to you
with nothing in return

But, instead, I choose to hold on to the precious
memories we were able to create
The brief moments when I was important enough to be a
part of your life

Those moments where your choice of poison didn't have
you tight in its grips
And you actually saw me and loved me

There were beautiful moments when I felt like you did
want to be a good father
So, I choose to hold on to those jewels and to whatever
love you were capable of giving me

I hold nothing against you as we all have our poisons
Yours was just more powerful than my love for you
could ever be

For whatever reason, it's what you wanted and needed

in this lifetime
So, I will hold compassion and love for you because
that's what I need in mine

Though this void is deep and wide, there is no room left
for anger or hate
Instead, it will serve as a constant reminder of what
could have been but never will be

I will fill as much of this emptiness up with love and
memories
Even if most were from a lifetime ago

As you were slipping away, I told you I love you, always
have and always will
I told you I wanted comfort and peace for you as I've
watched you struggle emotionally and physically for so
damn long

I can only hope you heard my words and felt my soul
reaching out for yours one last time
My hope is you finally allowed yourself to feel
unconditionally loved

Together, in this lifetime, we didn't get the chance to
heal and reconcile
And so our story may go unfinished...

But, regardless of the distance there was and the
vastness there is now
Your memory will always be a reminder that you're still
a part of me and I of you

# 5. Dragon-ing

I feel the need to shed my skin
And who I thought I was
Allowing scales of wisdom to cascade across my body
To break out of my shell and expand possibilities
To fill the cracks of hurt
Embracing my flaws and imperfections
Let my wings spread and carry me through the night
away from ancient skies
Stars lighting my path, removing shadows of the past
Breathe fire on all that no longer serves me:
things, man, ancestral chords...
Watch it all burn down with who I thought I was
and watch the ashes of those reflections
float away...
Letting it all burn a new path to self realization and self
love
To new wisdom if given the chance to cultivate
Feel myself soar to new heights as I rise above the pre-
conceived ashes
Uncharted feelings and emotion tattooing my rebirth
with reminders of lessons learned
To step forward and really breathe again
Let my heart beat and feel what it hasn't been allowed to
feel

Be free to be who I truly am
My beautiful authentic self
Be strong enough to know who she is
And embrace her in ways she hasn't been before
Have the courage to be her
Believe in her-
Her fierceness, her true strength, her intelligence, and her beauty
To love her
To truly love me

# 6. Africa is Poetry

Africa is poetry...

There is prose in every sunrise and sunset as golds paint the land, casting an eerie but beautiful radiant glow everywhere it touches. The moon gathers the light from the stories made and told during the day. Then, reflecting back its song to the sacred earth. Africa is poetic in the way the insects and birds sing over verdant land, home to a rainbow of life and colors. It's also in the way rivers and streams quench the growing crops' thirst.

Africa is poetry...

People
Vibrant, diverse
Home to lively spirits
Resilient, strong, filled with pride
Hopes, dreams

Stop, breathe
And hear their songs
Traditions passed through time
Whisper of their ancestors
Life blooms

Africa is poetry…

**A** vast land rich in uniqueness and culture
**F**lourishing with diversity in perfect harmony
**R**hythms of stories of yesterdays and today
**I**nviting all to share and be a part of its
**C**onnections of life and love
**A**llowing one's self to be transported back in time while
also living in the moment

Africa is poetry…

Africa is life
Tales of sorrow, triumphs
Acceptance with love

It is poetic
It is the haiku of life
The songs of wisdom

Africa is the true
Heart of the whole world
In all its glory

Trees and grass whisper
As the wind blows through fields

Finally, it rains

Their hope emanates
With every call of the wild,
Sunrise, and moonrise

Africa is poetry...

Africa comes alive with every heartbeat and breath
taken. It speaks of stories of the past, life of today, and
the dreams of tomorrow. Pain and sorrow is washed over
with love and unimaginable strength. Yet, it's not
forgotten. Ancestral shadows filled with lessons. Africa
is poetry in the tales of their ancestors, the strength of
their people, the call of the hawks, in the flowers that
line the streets, in the rain that quenches the earth, and
in the mighty trumpet of the elephant. Africa is sacred
and a part of us all.

Africa is poetry...

# 7. Your Warm Embrace

Every morning when I wake up,
after whispers of your love filled my slumber,
a comforting warmth envelops me
and I feel fortunate to see you lying beside me.
Bathed in the sun's gentle light,
casting an angelic glow upon your form.
Shadows dance around us
and trees sway
    back and forth
back and forth
    back and forth
 to the music of the wind.

Mornings like this bring a smile to my face
as clouds quickly gather.
Small raindrops begin to fall
and thunder
    softly calls out across the sky
urging me to linger in bed a moment longer,
Next to you,
snuggled in your warm embrace.

When you awaken, I see all the love in your eyes
And I wonder, "How am I the one?"...

Through the lows and highs,
failures and triumphs;
and after all the
        could-haves,
        should-haves, and
        would-haves;
You still choose me.
And, I, forever choose you.
You still move my heart
        with every look,
        every touch,
        and every thought...
You make the butterflies fly
and the goosebumps race.
My love for you deepens.

You tell me things,
        show me things
        whisper things
not that are solely beautiful,
        but that are sincere.
With you, I find my solace,
the place I feel most at peace.
Next to you I feel safe.
And, in your arms is where I feel complete.

On days the wind howls too loud

or lightening strikes a little too close,
when the creeks swiftly swell
making me feel like I'm drowning,
when insecurities loom large
and I feel like I can't do anything right,
through the challenges and mistakes,
when things don't go as planned;
You are always there to love me.
Embracing me with your gentle hands.

Whether we watch a comedy in bed
or explore the world,
Whether we bask in the sunlight
or dance in the twilight's glow,
if time were to separate us and I had to find you;
I'd search the whole Universe through and through
until our souls were reunited.
Dreams upon dreams,
    wishes upon wishes
Your warm embrace is where I always want to be.

# 8. Finding a Lost Poet

She does't know where she is going or even why.
Yet, the stars keep pulling her along,
    softly and warmly.
And in her soul,
she knows this is a journey she must take
To allow her heart to beat again and every part of her
feel.
To free her soul and escape from the confines of what
she thought kept her safe,
To feel what has been locked up inside for a moment too
long,
    and give it wings to fly.
To breathe again and break from the suffocation as she
steps forward into the light.
Shadows fade and paths glow with every new step she
takes.
A bioluminescence of life left to experience,
Whispers of doubt silencing and waning into the past.
Her heart guides her with its rhythmic beat,
Her mind dancing with newfound strength and courage.
She gathers pieces of memories and forgotten dreams,
Scattering into the wind those that no longer serve her,
    and perhaps never did.
Moonlight guides her to stories waiting to be told

and words left to be written.
To paths she never knew existed or was too afraid to
take.
As she makes her way through,
darkness turns to light
Igniting a fierceness in her she didn't know she had.
The world unfolds as colors vibrate around her
Energy moving in and out.
She has finally been set free,
Her soul now flowing like a river, unbound
A poet no longer lost.

# 9. You're Gone

It has been a month since you left.
But this time,
     you're really gone.
And it's so strange to me when I see you in my mind
Thinking you'll still be there when I get home,
Thinking there's still Time,
     a chance
That we can heal our broken relationship.
At least talk.

But, you're gone
And you're not coming back.
Not like when I was younger and you would leave
For days,
     weeks,
     months,
or even a year at a time
And, then, out of the blue,
     you'd be back.
As if nothing ever happened
As if everything was ok
Until the wind carried you away again.

It has been a month

and the thought of you
        sometimes haunts me.
Because I will never know or get the chance to see-
If we could have had a good relationship at some point,
If we could have come together and talked it out,
If we could have shared a loving embrace...
But none of that will come now
Because you're gone.


They say time heals all
But I think I still need more...
Because I still feel pain and hurt
Deep veins filled with rushing emotion
Filled with words unsaid
Words that now linger
        in the wind.
Because you're gone
You're really gone.

# 10. Ethan: A Beacon of Resilience and Passion

In the heart of a young boy named Ethan,
Is a son of enduring courage and strength,
Embracing change and transformation,
Your soul a balance of peace and grace.

Deep brown eyes, windows to your soul,
Reflect love, loyalty, and determination.
A spirit that is independent and enduring,
You balance your world with understanding wisdom.

On the soccer field you shine bright,
Gracefully gliding across the pitch.
With passion for life and the game you adore,
Your essence a reminder of the beauty in resilience.

Protective and emotional, yet strong and firm,
Loving and comforting in your presence.
Communicating with ease and a laugh that's infectious,
You're a Gemini at heart, quick-witted and curious.

A warm smile lighting up the darkest of days,
With confidence you walk through life.
Nurturing those around you with fearless love,

You're a beacon of hope and light.

Oh Ethan-Boy, with a heart of gold,
Rare like Alexandrite, with passion that shines.
Your spirit unyielding, a soul so pure,
You're our cherished pride in the tapestry of life.

# 11. Spirits of the Land

Spirts lay in the fields of Rwanda
Filled with sorrow of pain that runs deep
Among the verdant lands
Innocent lives were taken
Families were destroyed
Their dreams of a better life, shattered

Driving by I hear the cries of past memories
Women losing their husbands, babies, and innocence
Fathers losing hold of the ones they loved
Screams heard through the Land of a Thousand Hills
Tears filling rivers turning them red
Hearts broken as souls were savagely taken

My heart aches for the souls lost,
That wander aimlessly in haunting whispers
My heart aches for the living
I see the pain swirling in your eyes,
But I also see their spirits living in your smiles
Accepting and loving because we are all one

The spirits of this beautiful land are strong
No matter the past, you push forward
Working tirelessly day in and night out

Standing together in justice and in grace
From the ashes, stronger spirits arose with love and
acceptance
Your undying strength is truly inspiring

# 12. The Truth About Unicorn Moms

There's a misconception about Unicorn Moms;
Perhaps not the whole truth is known.
They're funny, they're loving, they're silly—
Their hearts are known to be pure and strong

It's true they aren't perfect
But who is or wants to be, anyway?
Sometimes they sip a bit too much wine,
Or need a lot of strong coffee to start their day.

They may sing a little too loud at karaoke
Or shyly hide away in the background.
They may prance down the streets in their onesie
pajamas,
Or dance all night to music and laughter's sound.

They may temporarily borrow a kids' bike
Just to try out his obstacle course.
Then abandon ship and run quickly through the night,
Laughing loudly with zero remorse.

A Unicorn Mom may bake a cake,
Then throw some at the birthday girl.

Together they'll hold hands as they tumble down
Laughing hysterically, their bodies in a curl.

They may walk up together dressed in costumes,
To pick their kids up from school on Halloween.
Why not make them laugh and smile,
Even if others don't always agree?

They may stay up a little too late,
Talking and laughing together.
They may never be on time for anything,
No matter the time they decide to gather.

One may help heal your soul with goat yoga.
And, with gentle words they'll all heal your heart.
With energy work, one will help heal your body.
Unicorn Moms will love you no matter what.

They will bring you a sense of wholeness,
Reminding you that you're never alone.
Delivering groceries when illness strikes,
And safely bringing your children home.

They will rejoice in your victories,
And support you when you stumble and fall.
Offering comfort in your darkest moments,
When it feels as though you cannot move at all.

Unicorn Moms may love their morning coffee
Or perhaps a mimosa or two.
They may act like teenagers when together.
But can be serious when they need to be, too

Even as they embrace their grace,
Their laughter may echo a bit too loud.
Yet judgement is absent in their space,
And no one stands alone in the crowd.

So, here's to all of my Unicorn Moms,
My life would be so boring without you!
Here's to always embracing and loving one another,
And, to a sisterhood that's sacred and true.

# 13. In the Land of a Thousand Hills, Live a Million Smiles

In the Land of a Thousand Hills
Where the sun kisses the earth
And greets the dawn with warmth
Where the birds alert to a new day
Unbridled by pain and sadness
Live millions of Rwandan smiles

Emerald hills rise above the cool morning mist
Telling of stories old and new
People set about their long day with children in tow
Trekking through faithful fields
Farming to feed their family
With smiles that light up their faces

Despite long hours under the sun
Voices unite in song and laughter
As the winding wind whispers its tales
They rest under the trees' shadows
Greeting all who walk by with respect
And the most genuine of smiles

In the Land of a Thousand Hills
Rwandans wear their hearts on their sleeves
They welcome all, same or different
With open arms, grace, and bright smiles
As they have felt true pain and sorrow
They choose to spread harmony and love

Every smile is a beacon of hope
A warm embrace on even the coldest of days
Filled with resilience and strength
Inspiring to all who witness this elegance
Igniting an infectious movement
The children's being the most beautiful

Rivers of reverence flow steadily
Of ancient voices with lessons learned
Memories in their hearts give way to resilient spirits
In their silence and strength
They hold their own close to their heart
Embracing Rwanda's spirit of love and devotion

As the sun sets and the moon rises
As the crickets and frogs orchestrate the night's music
They rest their heads gently
The light from their smiles still lingering
Promising a better tomorrow
In the Land of a Thousand Hills

# 14. These Green Eyes

These green eyes entice me with a fire that burns with
passion.
They hold onto me with such force they make me weak
breaking down my defenses and making me helpless.
I lose all control of
>       myself,
>> my thoughts,
>>> the way I feel,
>>>> my actions.

These green eyes hold me captive to something that isn't
there
>       or perhaps is.
A pseudo feeling...
I become hypnotized,
>       lost in a trance of emerald green sea,
lost in a place I once thought I knew,
>       but realized I don't.

These green eyes call out to me in a language never
heard before
with a spirit so fresh and pure that I become alive
>       for a moment...
I feel the air caressing me as if for the first time.

I see a new world, a new life I've yet to travel.

Inside these green eyes I see a beauty I didn't know
existed,
A beauty that supersedes even the most breathtaking
sunset.
This beauty takes my breath away and makes the
butterflies dance inside of me.
This beauty makes me want to give in to it all...

In these green eyes I search for the answers to the
questions I have no courage to ask.
If I did, I wouldn't look away.
If I had the strength I wouldn't let myself feel so weak
     in the waves of the green sea.
If I did,
     I wouldn't feel the way I do.

These green eyes of mine have taken me to another
world not yet touched or tasted.
A journey to come
     or perhaps a road not to be traveled.
My green eyes have shown me nothing but sincerity and
kindness
even in all its mystery and sexiness.
They make me feel special.

But really, these green eyes of mine are merely specs of
what really is.
Flecks that lay sporadic in thick fields of brown and
gold.
Each color a world of its own.
Each color begging me to explore its galaxy within these
hazel eyes.

# 15. To My Mother

To My Mother,
The one with the strong but gentle hands
With kind blue eyes who look for the best in others
Even though they're tired and weary from life's
challenges

To my mother whose spirit is strong, unraveled by life's
tribulations
Standing as tall as a fortress and staying brave through it
all
Unwavering love growing with each storm and sacrifice
made

To my mother whose eyes light up with laughter,
chasing off fears
Even in the face of apprehension and sorrow
Unknowns flowing down a river of patience and
perseverance

To my mother whose beauty blooms like a carnation
With a heart full of light and unconditional love
Exemplifying tenderness, purity, and faith

To my mother, a star steadfast and bright

Who did her best to guide my younger brother and I
With selfless days and sleepless nights

To my mother who is a one-of-a-kind piece-
A poem, a song, an inspiring timeless painting
A rare gem, special and valuable in every way

To my mother who is the true definition of strength
Never giving up, even when times were tough
Doing parenthood all on her own in the fortress she
created

To my mother who has always been there for me
Who loves her family with all of her heart and soul
And would do anything in the world to see them happy

To my mother, an amazing Grandmother who has been
there from the beginning
Getting on the floor to play with them as babies
And cheering them on with each new phase and
accomplishment

To my mother who I once merely saw as my mother
And my enemy during my teenage years
But, now see her as not only my mother but my best
friend

To my mother, parts of me are because of you
Thank you for all of the lessons you've taught me and
guidance you've given
Thank you for never giving up on me, even when I may
have been difficult

To my mother, thank you for accepting me for me
Believing me in all of my dreams and encouraging me to
keep going
But most of all, thank you for loving me

To my mother, I love you more than I could ever say

# 16. Dear Moon

Dear Moon:


Are you lonely up there in the vast sky,
wishing you had a friend?
Are you cold as you sit up high,
wanting a coat to keep you warm?
Do you enjoy all the twinkling stars around you,
absorbing their light and reflecting their shine?
Or does their light keep you from quieting your mind?
Do you bask in the warmth of the sun's glow
Or get annoyed by its fiery brightness?


As you peak your way to check on earth are you happy
or are you sad?
Are you disappointed in our progress or still holding out
hope humanity will come to its senses?
Do you cheer on those doing their part to keep earth
habitable?
Do you shut off your own emotions as you absorb the
energy from so many others?
Or, do you hold space for their loneliness, their worries,
their happiness, their love?
Do you transform the energy with the light of the sun?
Do you send it back down with a positive charge hoping

to change earth's activity?

Do you know how many people smile when they look
up at you?
Do you feel their love growing with your reflective
radiance?
Do you know how bright you shine for all the world to
see no matter your phase?
　　　Day or night, waning or waxing, full or new.
Do you know how appreciated you are?
How you leave the earth in awe and give people hope
where hope may have been lost?
Do you know your strength?
Standing on your own different from your surroundings.
Do you know how truly beautiful you are and the way
you make others feel energized?

We do.
We see you in all of your glory and resilience.
We see how you reflect the sun's candle casting a glow
on darkened paths,
Guiding life through the motions.
We see how by just being you, the waves ebb and flow
pushing energy in and out,
　　　shaping all life.
We see how you keep us grounded in all aspects,
preventing us from floating too high.

You are beautiful and magical.
And, we truly see you.


Love,
The World

# 17. Sebastian: A Light of Purity and Grace

A teenager with a heart as pure as the sea,
Is the sweetest of boys, Sebastian.
With loyalty in your veins and friendship in your soul,
And turquoise eyes filled with wisdom and passion.

Secure in your beliefs, soothing in your ways,
Power emanating from your gentle essence.
Venerated and revered by all who know you,
Spreading joy to others in your presence.

Respected for your wisdom, admired for your grace,
Your passion for life is far-reaching.
Each day a new beginning full of possibilities,
Your spirit ignites the hearts, inspiring each soul's
teaching.

Whether rounding bases or strategizing chess,
Or weaving melodies with the violin's embrace,
You embody elegance, composure, and growth;
A deep passion akin to the Pisces' sweet grace.

Shedding light of hope in a world often misunderstood,
Embracing new beginnings with a spirit so true.

Filling the universe with love in its purest form,
Reflected in sea-green eyes with the sky's gentle blue.

We celebrate you, a true gem among us,
An expression of all that is good and bright.
A rainbow baby, blessed with grace and elegance,
Forever cherished, a beacon of light.

# 18. Snowy Reflection

The snow falls
The ground glistens
The air is completely still
Not a sound to be heard
And, for a serene moment
I finally see my reflection

# 19. Aubrey: A Heart Full of Light and Love

In a world of chaos and uncertainty,
You shine, a beacon of light, pure and free.
Aubrey, our daughter, noble and true
With a delicate beauty and gold specked-eyes of blue

Creative and artistic, with a brilliant mind,
You dance through life, graceful and kind.
Your power lies in your gentle touch,
A sweet demeanor that means so much.

Reading books and drawing dreams,
Your tender thoughts flow like constant streams.
A rainbow baby born after a storm,
Nurturing and strong, your spirit is warm.

Independent and optimistic, you stand tall,
Your sweet nature embraced and cherished by all.
Like pink violets and amethyst hues
You bring beauty to all that you choose.

A Valentine gift, an Aquarian soul,
You know in your heart that the sky is the goal.
A wonderful dream with wisdom untold,

A best friend forever, a hand to hold.

With every step you take we will stand by your side,
And help you pursue the dreams you have in this life.
With love and admiration we hold you near,
Aubrey, our daughter, you are loved so dear.

# 20. Tears of Time

Sometimes I want to scream
And release all of the tears I have stored
Tears held on for too many reasons unknown
Protected by an ancient dam
I hear the creaks and cracks from centuries of too much
pressure
And I fear the dam of emotions will ultimately break
A breach of personal vulnerability
A cascade of ancestral emotion
And all would drown in it's raging path
It's said from destruction comes beauty
Old and dead give way to lush beginnings
Sprouting hope and love to be shared
But also kept sacred
Often from the deepest crevices, comes the rarest of
jewels
Jagged edges soften over earth's travels and time
Becoming polished and beautiful
Perhaps I should ride the waves of time
Tasting and feeling every last drop of pain
Allowing their tears and mine to fall and be felt, finally
So that they may be free
So, that I, can be free

# 21. Words to My Future Self

Look at you and how far you've come
A small town girl traveling the world
Living on dreams and courage
Bravely jumping into the unknown

You are beautiful, though time has left its mark
With lines of wisdom etched upon your face
Crows feet happily dancing at your eyes' corners
A testament to the laughter that has filled your life

Cheers to you and the woman you have become
Once fearful of others' opinions
You have learned to embrace yourself
Shedding the harsh self-criticism that once held you back

It took time to navigate through childhood traumas
But you emerged from the shadows
Stronger than ever imagined
Every step you took led you to this moment in life

Look at you, with your grey hair
Flowing gracefully down your back
Once worried about stretch marks

You see them as beautiful emblems of your grown
children

You were a wonderful mother, you still are
You're loving, supportive, and attentive
Your children are fortunate to have you
And now as a grandmother, you continue to shine

Cheers to the woman you have grown to be
A devoted mother and wife, surrounded by a beautiful
family
You kissed their pains away, comforted their fears
And embraced their dreams and triumphs

You gave all you were capable of giving
And did everything you possibly could
Even though you doubted yourself
There was never any need to worry

Look at you, living your best life
Surrounded by those you love
With a treasure trove of memories that bring you joy
Enough to last a lifetime

While you cannot change the past
Or reclaim lost time
You have captured moments beautifully

Creating a legacy that will endure

Cheers to you and the mistakes made along the way
Each lesson learned has shaped you into a better person
Though fear of failure once loomed large
Remember, that it is simply part of learning and growing

So, let go of worry and live freely
Indulge in one more piece of chocolate and glass of wine
Shout from mountain tops and dance in the rain
Sway to the rhythm of the wind

Cry in front of people, unashamed
And express happiness in your own way
Write to your heart's content for no one but you
And, know you were always seen